A Few Things You Would Know
If You Were God

By

Benny Ferguson Jr.

A Few Things You Would Know If You Were God
By Benny Ferguson © 2014

ISBN:
978-1-7354117-4-3

Published by: The Ferguson Company

Editor & cover design:
http://roxanec.wix.com/time-to-read.com

Welcome

The precision set at the foundation of the universe is not a secret. Nor is it only available to a chosen few. Specifics about creation, specifics about life and their inner workings, can set you free and allow you to turn your experiences around on a dime. Can you accept them? Will you allow them to penetrate the mind to a welcoming soul, transforming your being from the inside out? Will you give them a moment of trust in order to see with your own eyes? You have the chance now to test your faith.

Unity Is Your Blessing And Your Curse

Unity with the divine, such as the divine itself has been a perplexing notion of the physical realm from the moment conscious beings began to walk. The notion that the five senses which allow in information, are the only means of communication for a being who has a mind, who has dreams, and who has thoughts is insane. To think that the physical existence is the only existence of a being who can communicate with himself, inside of himself without words, is preposterous. You are not a physical being. You are a spiritual being. You are expansive without measure. You are fully connected to Source energy through and through. You have lived innumerable lives for the advancement and experience of your soul, and when those lives have yielded you the ultimate knowledge of Source, you will return to Source with the full knowledge of creation and experience, and then you will start over again.

Unity is the blessing of life eternal with all of creation. The notion of unity, energetically is a unison, a connectedness, a wholeness with all matter, all animate and inanimate objects. However, in this sense, unity is the expression and effect that your life has on the expression of your soul. Every thought that is fathomed, every thought that is received, every thought that penetrates into the subconscious mind has an effect on you. Every thought effects whether you are able to connect fully with your soul and allow your soul's full expression or not.

The road that you follow in life must be guided by the inward flow of inspiration and not the outward imposing of physical ideas, assumptions, and societal norms. The road that is specifically designed for your highest growth and expression is a path that must be trodden fearlessly, and the humble of heart made meek by their physical existence have a longer way to travel to find that path due to the lack of strength and resolve of mind.

4

It is a pity that so many have lost entire lifetimes because the human race has forgotten their purpose, their highest calling. It is a pity that sons and daughters have not realized that their earthly mother and fathers are only there for a season, their inner guidance persist for eternity. "Take the best, and leave the rest," is a grand axiom to follow if it could be conveyed to the child. Adults who have succumbed to the false ideas of the physical realm only have false ideas, false cares to pass along. Thus, the child, a spiritual being newly present in the physical realm begins their journey misguided.

So where are you? Are you following the misguided ideas of parents, of loved ones, of society as a whole? Are you suffering through a life that was imposed on you or are you fearlessly living life based on the notion of an inspired heart?

Are you reading this material with a critical, skeptical eye, or are you reading and feeling the exhilarating cry of your soul to let go of the trash that has cluttered your highest, fullest expression?

There is no doubt that you are capable of more, because there is always more. There is no doubt that a marvelous portion of riches, wealth, and abundance awaits you, for there is enough present for all. There is no doubt that the company you keep is influencing you; how you experience life, they always have. The question is, from here on out, who do you listen to. Do you continue to listen to the outside physical world, or do you oust the clutter and open up to the bigger, grander you that has been trying to communicate through the fog during your entire lifetime.

Unity with a knowledgeable Source is your power toward a magnificent outcome. Unity with a command center that already knows your highest purpose, and the path that yields your highest experience; unity with boldness, fearlessness for life that already exists within you, which is necessary for the living and the walking of your path, that is you.

All Teachers Have Presented A Practice For Reconnection To Source

The universal theme of all teachings that have come close to the essence of true human experience and reality have displayed a practice and not just a mere philosophy. The teachers of old, all who had a depth of knowledge and perception, had it developed from work they had done on the inside. From the secluded monks, to Christ, all had learned or spent so much time contemplating inwardly and deeply that they discovered profound wells of blessedness. They discovered immense understanding and connectedness to something much greater then themselves. They touched the essence of life and the breathless nature it creates in the first timer. This drove them to tell all that they could.

But they did not stop there, they all continued their practice, whether they were learned techniques or they just continued what they were doing. The fact of the matter is that there was a progression to their growth, a progression to the understanding, a progression to the knowledge that they were able to grasp and assimilate into their being without blowing a fuse. There is only so much a mind can handle at a time because of the neurological makeup of your physical being. So it takes time to process the mass of information which is now accessible to you and it must be linked to physical experience for understanding.

The practice on which you embark is first a gathering of information, possibly how and why. Once you have come to accept those two facets, the process is a letting go, an undoing of all that you have learned and believed to be true about yourself and about the world around you. It is a releasing of all the negative, unhealthy, ill producing ideas that are plaguing your life, creating less than desirable effects or holding you back from accomplishing the desires of your heart.

There is an innumerable mix of ideas that are passed and shared amongst human beings. Some are limiting and some are not. Some are paralyzing and some are not. It depends first on the ideas that are carried by those who were around you when you were growing up and by those who had the most influence on you. Second, it depends on the progression of your life's experiences. If you had dramatic encounters or tragic events occurring in your life, it is most likely they had an immediate effect on you, possibly causing you to create beliefs or dominant ideas on the spot, which still exist and are driving your thoughts and behaviors as they relate to life and events surrounding the tragedy.

The practice is a letting go. It is a releasing of all of the ideas, all of the misconceptions, all of the misguided perceptions that you are currently allowing to guide you. All ideas that separate you from your fellow human beings, separate you from your Source, your true self, and create negative ill effects in your life. All ideas that move you to anger, frustration and stress, separate you from your Source, and create negative, ill effects in your life. All ideas that cause you to wish negative effects on others separate you from your Source, and create negative, ill effects in your life. All ideas that are less than beautiful, less than love, less than appreciative, less than thankful, less than grateful, create negative, ill effects in your life, and it is your responsibility to curb this mindset, to release these ideas and replace them with ones that serve your highest purpose and allow the blessing of life to flow to and through you.

A tragedy is only a tragedy if you allow it to move you mentally from a place of health to a place of sickness, disease, and pain. A tragedy is only a tragedy when you internalize negative thoughts and beliefs about yourself or about life, based on the event, and allow those ideas to create a slug that affects multiple areas of your life negatively as a result. This is the true tragedy.

I bid you good day, and the will to challenge the ideas that drive you. Question their highest intention, and if they serve you, bless them. Allow them to grow and flourish. If they curse you, remove them, cut them away and replace them with the highest, most magnificent of thoughts and press them into your subconscious. Gratefully yours.

The Wealth Of Experience Lie In Their Feeling Nature

Physical experience is not the enormous question mark that it appears to be. There is no grand wielder of your life. There is no cosmic commander who is choosing your pains and your struggles. The Source of all creation is experiencing the edge of energy just as you are. Source is experiencing the edge of reality through you, as you. As a conscious piece and parcel of Source energy, you are choosing your experiences. You are choosing your future. You are choosing whether to stay physically where you are in life, or you are choosing to pull yourself out of the situation into a newer, higher plane. You are choosing. Yes, you are choosing.

So how and why are you choosing? Choice is the thought. Choice is the belief. But greatest of all, choice is the vibration. It is the energy that you present to the field which dictates the energy that the field presents back to you. It is the energy that you present to the field which dictates the nature of experience that you encounter. You may experience what some may call tragedy, but it will not be tragedy from your perspective. You may experience loss in relationship from the world's view, but it will not be relational loss from your perspective and therefore your energy vibration will not be affected.

The first quest for the individual human being is to train the mind at the subconscious level to seek out and maintain the highest states of vibration. That means only entertaining the highest possibilities, the highest outcomes, the highest experiences, the highest totals, the highest imaginable successes. If they are not reached, pull all of the learning they have to offer from each particular situation, integrate and assimilate them, and continue your journey of experience, growth, and expansion. This is your journey. This is the cycle, experience, growth, and expansion. Once you have the learning, reset yourself, reset your targets, reset your goal posts with expectation and knowing that the results you seek already exist, and continue your movement forward. That is it.

Yes, the wealth that exist in each and every experience lies in the experience's feeling nature. Connect with the feeling of the experience, the accomplishment, the success. Connect inwardly with the vibration, the energy, and allow it to guide your thoughts, your beliefs, your actions, your behaviors, and through the energy vibration, all of the doors that are required to open for materialization of your goal will be opened.

Nothing else exists but your goal. There is no other potential outcome but the success of your goal. You refuse to allow any other experience into your life except the accomplishment of your goal. Demand your goal to show itself because you know it already exist in a universe where all is already given. Claim your goal by not compromising mentally, emotionally or energetically. Know it just as you know your sun exists and shines whether you can see it or not. Know it!!!

Now, to the caveat. The caveat to all of this madness is that, in the end, you are the chooser. Source energy is experiencing the far edges of energetic reality through you as you. And as a conscious piece and parcel of Source, you are the chooser; you are the creator of the experiences around you. You are the one who allows. You are the revealer. You are the manifester. You are the materializer. You are the distinguisher between what the real is for you and what is not. Believe, intend, and know that your desires exist. Refuse to compromise with their materialization. Bathe in the energy vibration of their success, and you will have it.

There Is A Highest Position Of Choice At Every Moment

Moment by moment by moment, the choices that you make are the determining factors. It is no secret that the choices you make determine your life. It is no secret. To truly own the life which you are destined to live, you must own the choices you make on a moment by moment basis. Yes, this is true, but what do you choose?

You choose the highest, grandest, most glorious outcome and circumstance imaginable. That is what you choose. Mentally you are starving for the exhilaration of success and accomplishment, and you can have it by merely entertaining the thought. See your present situations at their highest peak, all resolutions materializing to the fullest. All relationships maintained at their most fulfilling level. All finances flowing in line with universal wealth.

There is a highest and best possible outcome for you at every moment, but you must see it, you must feel it, and you must live it as close to the truth of it as you can. Let every thought, every emotion, every word, every action be a claim to this truth as your reality.

In the defense of life itself, it will flow with or without your choice. The sequences of appearances as experience make no claim to responsibility for your feelings or the negative or positive contrast of the physical realm. There is only materialization. There is only manifestation in accordance to your chosen pattern of feeling. The highest thought, the highest choice, keeps you in line with vibration, the highest energy of love and kindness when success remains in your focus and is all encompassing.

In regards to the masses, the choice is the one which is accepted by most. The pains of the world are the norm. The constant mistakes of the world are the norm. The ever cycling replay of losses is the norm because of their choosing, their constant focus are the negative outcomes against which they fight, those from which they want so desperately to escape, those they abhor with all of their thoughts, energy and emotions. In this manner they (the masses) are passionately doing all the right things at the mental, energetic level, but in the wrong direction because their choice is the exact life situations and circumstances they do not want. Obvious, but not obvious at the same time, because they have no one to give them contrast.

You, my friend, now have the code. You have the conscious option of choice. You have met the key maker, the one who can open the doors to a successful, fulfilling life, and that person is you.

You do not have to trust. You do not have to believe. You must simply begin making a habit of choosing and maintaining your life in the highest regards, moment by moment. There is no one else but you. The universe of you consists of one person, everyone else are merely passersby.

Your Diamonds Are Often Disguised In Mud

Mistake!

One of the most critical mistakes of human beings is to misplace the meaning of their experiences.

1. There is no good or bad experience. It is merely experience; experience with which you have aligned yourself.
2. The quicker you begin learning from your experiences, the quicker you will begin removing yourself from the level of vibration that created the experience in the first place.
3. The idea that pain or discomfort is bad is a weak, faulty view of life. The truth is that pain and discomfort have always been a part of the mechanism of growth, more so the discomfort, not pain. Growth can be uncomfortable. Expansion can be unsettling. Frustration and chaos are excellent indicators that greater understanding, awareness, and growth are on the horizon. Frustration and chaos are great indicators that you are on the path to becoming more than you are right now.

So what have you gleaned from your life to this point? What have you grabbed from the jaws of failure and mistake? The masses have resolved to become victims of circumstances. They find themselves stuck in the moment, regretting, angry, and convinced that the world owes them payment for their effort. All the while they continue to draw and attract the pain as a result of their focus and clarity being directed on the experience which is creating their suffering. They believe that experience has been cast upon them, and undeservedly feel the right to the anger they display.

Their lives are cursed, and they are the curse. Their belief in the victimhood, pain, weakness, and suffering is their curse, and it will plague their lives until they grasp firmly that the learning they seek, the understanding they seek is right beneath them. It is swirling around them, and is available to them the very moment they turn

12

their attention, their focus from what appears to be a problem, to growth and expansion.

Great clarity to life can be found in devastation. Clarity of focus can be found in loss. Jewels of direction can be found in what appears to be uncalculated, unexpected changes in life's circumstances. The commitment to discovering what life is offering you for your soul's journey is critical to uncovering your path. It is, as they say, "The Secret."

To what do you owe this grand opportunity? To what do you owe the offering of great understanding and clarity? You owe nothing. Your greatest blessing to the gift of experience is to maintain the perspective of growth and expansion. Within your greatest pain and within your greatest accomplishment, meticulously look and pull all that is obvious and not so obvious for growth and integration into your being.

1. What did I learn about the process?
2. What can I do next time that may provide a greater result?
3. How did I feel during the process? Was fear a guiding principle at any point? Where did the fear come from? What idea do I focus on in the next experience to negate the idea of fear?
4. What is the next logical, highest experience toward which my soul is drawing me?
5. Where is the energy of my soul leading me?
6. How much more can I handle as responsibility?
7. What effect did my command of me have on my experience?
8. Where do I go from here in my quest of greater experience, growth, and expansion?

These are just a few questions that will get you percolating on the meaning and the learning available to you.

Yes, you can become more at every moment, or you can remain stagnant in a painful, suffering environment and existence because the cycle of thought and belief holds you bound. There is no cycle when your trajectory is up; there is only attraction and greater, more expansive experience.

I bid you good day.

The Need For Courage Represents A Belief In Fear – Pure Activity Is Impartial

Why do you need courage? The only reason a human being would need courage is if that individual believed in its polar opposite, which is fear.

Every concept, every idea that is manifest in the physical realm has its polar opposite, has its contrast. There is no light without dark. There is no day without night. There is no up without down. There is no good without what appears to be not so good. These events or different experiences provide you with contrast for greater, higher choice of experience.

In the experiences of your life, in your relationship, finances, health, in your mental activity, the experiences that appear less than what you would actually choose, serve to provide you with greater clarity and sharpened focus. Their reason is not to bring you pain and suffering, for if you are focused on the next plane, on higher, on more, you are constantly onboard the mechanism of growth and therefore riding a forward wave of excitement.

However, merely recognizing contrast, and believing in the circumstances that appear around you are two different things. Your belief in lack makes it a permanent part of your financial experience. Your belief in sickness makes it a permanent part of your health experience. Your belief in the negative behaviors of people makes their potential darkness a part of your relational experience.

However, the first belief to quell, which provides the launching pad for success, resides in seeing the fault of all other faulty beliefs, is the idea of courage. The acceptance of the idea of courage indicates your belief in the idea of fear. Because you believe in the idea of fear, you feel as though you need its polar opposite to counter it. Neither is real. To believe in one means you are constantly engaged in a tug of war between the two ideas. This most often leaves you paralyzed, motionless, with the activity required to move you toward accomplishment being left undone.

Nature, does not entertain fear or courage. There is only activity. There is only movement forward. There are only the necessary actions, the necessary steps to take. In some instances, there is danger, but danger requires certain actions to be taken as well. This is the true state of your being. You are active. You are engaging. You are overcoming. You are creating. You are experiencing, and if you are not doing these things on an ever increasing, bigger and higher scale you are not following or growing at the pace of your soul's purpose. Fear lives somewhere within you and is stifling your true being. It is stifling the free, full expression of you.

Fear, is an idea, an expectation or an anticipation of pain that creates great conflict on the inside of the individual human being. It had its birth many years ago during the creation of the conscious, thinking mind. Many of your strongest leaders have discovered its power and used it to command and control huge masses of people as a whole. These leaders have stifled creativity. They used the idea of potential pain and suffering to block the spirit of free expression, and today, this activity continues to play a part in your life. The idea of fear casts an immense shadow, a fog over your entire life, and you do not realize that shining light on the idea of fear reveals an entire different, more powerful existence beyond its borders.

You have a choice, as is the major theme of this series, to confront fear as it appears around every corner. You have a choice, if not in your physical activity, at least in your mental activity. Box it in, question it, and notice its lack of truth. Notice its illusory nature in the present moment. Notice in your past how it has halted your movement. Notice how its presence throws your inner activity awry, stopping all possible outer, physical activity.

The mind is its own weapon, and over the years of human existence it has become its own enemy. Become acutely aware of the false images that are presented to you by your mind. Become acutely aware of the costs that have mounted in your life as a result of its presence and false activity. Make a resolute determination no longer to allow the marching warriors of you to be stopped by the nameless,

16

motionless fog. Wisk fear away and continue forward with the pure, impartial activities of your heart.

The Death Of You Today Will Lead To New Life Tomorrow

Death in the physical sense is a very natural event, a transition back to the energy realms for processing and integrating of the experiences you encountered. It is also a time of reuniting with old friends and family, those closest to you and those watching over you now.

If you are reading this material, you are in a place of personal discovery, personal awakening, and the death to which we refer in the title is not one of physical exit, but one of mental exit. The cancellation of your "old life" now relies upon learning and upon your ability to begin making the necessary corrections to your frame of thinking. It can be directly related to a death of sorts because it is an ending of the old you, your old patterns of thought, your old dominant ideas or beliefs, your old emotional patterns, your old speaking habits, and your old behaviors. It is an ending point and a beginning. It is a beginning of new energetic patterns that correct many faulty functions of the body. It is the beginning of new experiences in life, narrowing your focus to the truth of what are your responsibility and your capability in creation and experience. It is a beginning to the new plateaus to accomplishment that are available to you. It is a beginning to the authenticity and to free self-expression that opens the door to your soul's path, its original design for your life.

Commonly known as the "Accidental Wave," is the progression of thought energy into negative or ill-fated scheduling of experience. It is upon these mistaken hills of thoughts that the hated occurrences, the disastrous occurrences, the destructive occurrences of your life are built on. Each one spiraling you further and further into despair, into patterns or realms of thoughts that cement you into the pain and suffering that exists for those who refuse to place their perspective on the highest of potential, the highest of possibility.

Death is a must. It is necessary. Let it all go. Begin anew with a blank slate. Freshen your eyes and see all that is available, not just to what you are experiencing now, but to what others have experienced as well. What separates one human being's experience from that of another? Their personal, individual patterns of thoughts are all that separates one from another. It is all that separates you from the life that you imagined as a child. It is all that separates you from the fame, from the travel, from the love, from the power and from the respect you deserve, need and want. It is all that separates you from whatever it is that drives you to accomplishment and toward the fulfillment that lies along the path that is your life. It is all there, for whatever is there that you feel is uniquely you.

Free yourself from all negative, painful thoughts. Allow the past to lie in the grave of experience, and allow it to give you the clarity of what you like and desire in the world. Make your past a playground of discernment. Make it an experimental chamber of sorts, a place where you make moldings of the life you desire based on the contrast of the life that you have already experienced. It is a beautiful process, one that immediately shows the potential of a shift in focus.

We honor you for your endeavor in this track of understanding. It was our honor and privilege to serve you on your quest to make personal responsibility and brilliance your life of choice.
Namaste

Absolute Commitment Makes The Chosen Result A Certainty

Reality as a whole does not have chaotic effect to its nature. Nothing in reality is chaotic. Everything exists with precision and presence, with a purpose and with a cause. If something goes out of balance there is a rebalancing. If something is forced out of order, there is a reordering. With precision your planet hangs in relationship to your sun and the moon. The minutest adjustment would equal the destruction of your race and your planet as you know it. So, with this known, what makes you think that your life is a random list of events and happenings that either serve to bring you joy or serve to bring you pain.

No, the same precision that exists in the natural order of your world and the universe is present in your daily life. Reality, as you see and experience it, is a result of a cause. That cause is you. You are the center of your universe. You are the constant, the sun, around which all of the happenings in your life experience orbit and propel.

The unified truth of the human existence has been seen throughout time, and can be observed easily in the lives lived by many of the most exceptional human beings. That unified truth is that absolute commitment makes your chosen result or reality a certainty. Absolute commitment makes the statement to your subconscious mind that you wholly believe in the experience you seek. Absolute commitment makes the statement, that there is no other outcome and that you have collapsed all possibilities down to one highest, ideal possibility for you. Absolute commitment sets your intention and your focus firmly on the prize with the knowledge that it is possible and that it exists because you see it firmly in your mind.

Commitment has taken a bad rap because so many have claimed to commit to goals and dreams, and the minute they fall short or come up against a setback they retreat or drop their pursuit all together. Absolute commitment requires a state of mind whereby there is no retreat, there is no turning back. It is not an option. It is not an available choice. There is only success. There is only achievement. There is only the goal or the experience.

To each is their own interpretation of the law, but it is law nonetheless. The showing of your belief in truth is evidenced in your actions. It is evidenced in how your respond to the appearance of remnants of the thought energy you entertained, which was based in fear and anxiety, the obstacles that you foresaw, based on your lack of belief in free flowing success.

Trust in the process. Trust in the precision that exists, the precision that holds all in balance. Trust that your commitment, absolutely, mentally and energetically, will yield a rebalancing, a manifesting in the physical realm.

Your ability to create, to manifest, is not a question of possibility, it is a question of commitment, belief, and focus.

Belief In The Past Commits The Greatest Of Sins

Sin, yes sin, is nothing more than those thoughts that separate you from the highest, purest Source energy. Forgiveness is merely a resetting of mind (mentally and emotionally) to the corrected state of connection and wholeness with your Source.

The gravest of sin, the gravest of separations from Source that tend to swell and fester is the belief in your past. This is the downward spiral of all who would-be heroes, champions, or saviors. It is the rickety bridge that all who believes in their past refuse to cross for fear of falling through the cracks. The past of any individual human being can be likened to quicksand, for the more a person struggles, wrestles with the events in their past, the deeper they sink into the original pain and suffering that was caused as a result of these events.

The past, your past, is a historical event that has no relevance or power over your present moment, except for that which you give it. It does not matter how painful, how tragic the event may have been, its effects do not have to have bearing on your life as it presents itself now.

The past, as you know it, is a sprinkling of peppered festering, here and there. Occurrences that left you scared, and left you strengthened. Your past is full of events that you regret and that you wish would have extended into your present. No matter the nature of the events in your past, their only return possible is triggered by the energy and focus that you give them mentally. This is why the gravest of sins is the belief in your past.

As long as you harbor the pain, you give it life in the present moment, and continue to project it forward into your future. That is number 1. Number 2: if you have anyone who looks to you for guidance, you are passing on the belief in the pain to them as well, setting them up unconsciously for the same pain and suffering that continues to repeat itself in your life. Number 3: you are failing to exercise your ability to choose. You have the ability to choose a

22

different perspective of the event. You have the ability now to view the event from more experienced, learned eyes and make new, higher interpretations, altering your present mental and emotional states related to the events.

Choice is the monument that will not be overlooked when command of your life is sought after. Choice is the multileveled faction that when engaged refuses to give less than its calling.

An eagerness to release the past amplifies the options that are available and brings them into plain sight. Once in sight, the choices are clear; if the highest and best creates a shift in the mental and emotional realm of the individual, it will produce the greatest return on effort and personal adjustment.

Common to most is viewing the past as permanent and inescapable. This could not be further from the truth. All human experiences can be experienced by all. All human experiences can be released by all. There is no permanent or inescapable when it comes to human experience or the human condition. There is only choice and the past has no bearing whatsoever on your choice.

Weathering The Storms Of The Present Moment, Grant Empowerment & Endurance For Future Endeavors

Akin to many great adventurers, to many great explorers, the greater the experiences in which you place yourself, the broader your potential and your abilities become.

Do not shy away from the problems or the challenges of your life. Meet them head on with vigor and passion, believing there is resolution and growth to be found at their center, specifically for you. This includes your relationships, health, and your financial situations. The goal, however, is to transcend the reactionary form of life and move to a proactive, choice frame of mind and experience.

At present, the masses cycle through multiple recurring life experiences because they refuse to take responsibility for their actions. They refuse to see that the nature of life is to experience, grow, and expand. Evolution proves this. The development of the human mind from a babe to adulthood proves this. All animals prove this when placed in situations that are new or foreign to their norm. They adapt, they grow, and they assimilate the new information and develop new trains of thought based on the new input. As human beings, who tend to get stuck in certain frames of thinking, you fail to do the same.

You fail to adapt. You fail to learn. You fail to grow, and as a result you continue to experience the same or similar results over and over again in every area of your life. This is interesting because in your sporting events, and in business, you are highly aware of your results. You are constantly gathering new information as they are presented by your experiences. You use that information to gauge whether you are closing in on the success that you seek. If not, you adjust, you gain new skills, you get help, and you do this over and over until you reach your goal of success.

However, in the critical areas of relationships, personal finances, health, and even in the growing of your spiritual connection to your Source, you fail to employ the same tactics. You are comfortable with the acceptance of your fate of loss and despair, because you feel as though you have no control over the human factors involved. You are correct, you do not have control, but you do have control over the light of energy in which these human factors appear throughout your life.

Contrary to your present beliefs, the life experiences you choose right now hold massive value for you and for your life. The wealth of knowledge and understanding available to and for you, and only you, in these experiences is immeasurable. The shift that must occur is the shifting of your focus from the world's reactionary, victim perspective, to a proactive, accepting viewpoint.

You already have the tools available to you to extrapolate the knowledge necessary to propel you up and out of the cycle of your present experiences. You must begin to use them in the right frame of mind. When you do this, the experiences of your life will begin to become launching pads for greater growth and expansion.

The Inner Clock Already Knows When The Bell Will Toll; Live Your Gifts Now

The most valuable treasures are those tangible aspects of you that cannot be removed, and continuously desire to be expressed and realized.

The adult human being knows of the tangible aspects, the inner voice, and the urgings that I speak of. It is the desired movement toward a particular experience. It is the urge to be surrounded by a certain type of people. It is the desire to drive a certain type of car, to wear certain clothes based on what they represent to you.

It is the draw to certain careers and certain types of experiences for entertainment. It is the repulsion of other experiences because they are not a part of your inner magnetic makeup or calling.

To the attuned, there is a passion or depth of feeling that accompanies those experiences which fall in line with the path of an individual's soul. There is excitement. There is a feeling of flow. There is a true sense of purpose.

Your gifts, the areas of life that come easiest to you; the endeavors in which you excel; the areas of study you are enjoying the most; the things you do or enjoy doing that allow you to bring joy to yourself and others are your blessings from Source. They are the basis of what could be your contribution to the world and your ability to touch lives.

Many have projected themselves onto the wall of fame in your history, based on what seemed to be menial likes or patterns. From cooking recipes, to buying property, to singing and writing songs, each individual has the ability to affect others to a higher more enjoyable state of mind, but you do this with the highest power behind you, when you are using your natural born tools to the best of your ability.

There is no conscious knowing when the opportunity you now have will expire. So it is critical that you begin employing your best tools, your strongest assets in the battle of living, gaining success, and affecting lives.

The truth is that until you are fully engaged in realizing your beauty, and the magnificence of your gifts, you are not fully living.

Quickly practice to highlight your gifts. Recognize them, notice how allowing them to flow affects those around you, and figure out how to align yourself with or create a career that allows you to express those gifts fully.

The true death of an individual human being is the slow, subtle moaning and grumbling of a soul that has yet to be expressed. There are regrets. There are unfulfilled desires waiting to be tapped. There are people with whom you identify, but you are scared to release and really live that side of you into the world, and it is painful. You experience nightmares of repression, nightmares metaphoric of freedom and release. You experience nightmares of a looming ending for which you are not ready. This is death, but it does not have to be you. You can sever the fear. You can release the concern for what others think, and begin to live your life, truly live, and express your soul's purpose.

Disaster Is A Balancing Of The Earth & A Movement Energy

Mankind has long lost its focus, and has become fixated on the outside, physical realm of energy. It is the last level of manifestation of so many levels that emanate from Source. This fixation has only been a point of confusion, and has served to dishearten because it appears to be only a plane of disaster, mishaps, and tragedy. This it is not. Again, it is the outer realm of existence. Its natural activities are the result of inner causes that bubble into effects in the outside world.

It is a process, an occurrence very similar to that of the activities of the human body, or that of a volcano. With the body of a human being, the mindset or habitual thought patterns, and the emotional thrust assisting those thoughts create huge movements in the body and yield the behaviors and experiences which are seen and felt in the environment. Similarly, the volcano is a deep pit of boiling and churning energy until all of this hidden activity explodes to life and erupts, ejecting its lava onto the environment. Both are the same process. The activities that you see, the outward displays are the last segment. They are the ultimate result of inner activities. They are the result of the inner driving force. The lion on the plains of Africa that attacks a young wildebeest does so after decisions made inwardly drive them to that activity. All of creation is an outward result of inner movements and processes. The natural activities of the world, the activities that you call disaster and tragedy are not different.

Earthquakes, landslides, hurricanes, typhoons, tornados, and the lot, are all results of inner activities. They all exist as a part of the mechanism, the organism that you call your planet, and they all participate in balancing the energies that flow constantly just beyond the observing ability of your eye. Yes, radio frequencies exist. Yes, light rays exist. Yes, powerful electric currents course through your skies with incredible velocity and destructive, creative strength. That energy is present at every moment. They become visible, or their activity becomes obvious when large amounts of this energy meet one another or collide. This balancing out of the energies, a smoothing out of their flow, and this inner activity has definite observable, outer physical realm effects.

Are these activities good or bad? No, they just are, and any human or animal life that is transitioned as a result of this activity, whether it is one or many, is a soul's calling home. This means that they were at the appropriate time at the appropriate place for that appropriate reason, transition.

The activity of the human body is no different. The energies that the masses entertain thoughtfully and emotionally are the causing force behind many of the unhealthy activities that exist in the world. The breakdown of relationships, of family, and of the physical health of the body, the onslaught and experience of sickness and disease are the result in large part of the plane of energy in which many human beings now participate. The negative, angry, vengeful, jealous, regretful energies that affect the body inwardly flow in the world with disastrous outward results. All negative, low energy thought and emotion is a destructive force on your body. It weakens. It confuses. It frustrates. It divides. It creates conflict, and becomes your demise.

You allow these energies to exist. You perpetuate their existence by holding on to their memory. You contribute to the pain and suffering of the world by believing the existence of these negative low vibrating energies to be normal and inescapable. All of these are lies that you have fallen for hook, line, and sinker.

You are the chooser, and choice is your greatest asset. Yes, the energies exist, and they always will, but you choose in which to participate. You choose which you will allow to flow through your existence and your experience. Choice is your weapon in creation and materialization, and a powerful weapon it is.

Crystallizing Your Thoughts Around The Highest Ideas Transform Your Life

There is no experience beyond your reach. It is all a matter of your drawing and participating in the energies that are necessary to eventuate its arrival. It requires you to be the energy. It requires you to be the experience. It requires you to acknowledge its existence as being real with a powerful uncompromising knowledge, before the experience is received and acknowledged by your five senses.

The process to transform any area of your life that you wish to see improvement is a simple one. However, it requires discipline and consistency. This process is to claim mentally and emotionally the highest idea. It is to claim the highest visual and emotional experience. It is to claim the highest vibrational connection to the highest imaginable end.

Think of a child's approach. The creation of a new game is approached with excitement and vigor. The details of the game have yet to be worked out but the incredible experience that the game will deliver is already being felt and experienced by its creators. This pulls the details through into materialization smoothly and quickly. The creators are already feeling the game. They are living the game. They are the game!

This is the process, and it has not changed even though you, as an adult, have lost faith in its effectiveness. You have lost faith in its validity. You believe that you must work endlessly to force the occurrence of your desired result but, in the end, you really have no control. This is a sad outcome for one who started out their physical existence so powerful and with so much promise.

When was the last time you entertained your ideal state of experience in any area of your life? When was the last time you took a moment to describe to yourself what you want, and did this devoid of any ideas of experiences that you do not want? For the masses this is rarely the case. They are too wrapped up in reacting to the negative consequences of their inner activity to step back and consider the following:

- What do I want my experience to be?
- Who do I need to be to create this experience around me?
- How does it feel to have the experience?
- How exciting is it for this to be my normal experience?
- How does it feel for the negative outcomes to be a distant memory?
- What would be the steps that I would suggest to anyone desiring to overcome or change the experiences that I have overcome or transformed?

These are powerful questions that put you in a transformative state of mind. To question how you would educate and empower someone else to overcome the situation that you have/are overcoming, is one of the most transformative processes there are to personal, individual change.

So if you could choose, wouldn't you choose the highest, most grand, most fascinating outcome available and possible? You can begin to choose mentally and emotionally now, knowing and with faith that all inner works becomes outer experiences. The more you entertain the thought, the more the thought and all that is required for its materialization becomes who you are, and when you are the person who experiences that which you seek, you have it.

Mass Mind Reveals The Fault Of Man, Go Opposite & Be Free

The mind of mankind has been on a steady decline since the beginning of time. The outside carries with it such fascination, such beauty, so many opportunities to experience and grow beyond the present condition that man has forgotten to look inward for their strength and guidance in these endeavors.

The question for the one who is seeking, the question for the one who is aching for understanding is, "What are those who have reserved themselves to silence and stillness looking for? What are they finding?" If you look down through your history, in the spiritual dimensions and teachings of your race, you will find those who have stumbled upon the profound. You will find those who have stumbled upon inner wealth and abundance. Once they recognized what they had or were on the verge of doing, they never let it go. This is the mistake of man. The knowledge of other human beings who have formed a conviction around their practice of inner awareness and inner investigation at least deserves some attention. It is still free for the ones who wish to venture and discover their inner being.

Mass mind with its ideas, its beliefs, its values, its preconceived notions, its misguided suggestions, and its faulty routines, only provides proof to the truth of the ill fates of the world. Mass mind and its full knowing and belief only in that which it can experience with its five senses, is a doomed position to expect constant outcomes from others.

Mass mind is a continuous falling into detrimental and ill-fated situations due to the fact that the expectation of negative consequences and experiences only leads to greater negative consequences and experiences.

You now have the opportunity to turn away from the mind of man. You have the opportunity to go opposite of all that you see and believe to know, that does not serve you, excite you, or move you toward greater experience, growth, and expansion.

32

The cardinals of past leadership shunned greater experience because it always resulted in a broadened mind, and a broadened mind was always a threat to the norm. It was also a threat to any system of control using fear to command the minds and behaviors of human beings.

So growth was out. Expansion was out, and the attempt at either was frowned upon. This is not the case now. With so much information available to you it is hard to know where to start. The answer to that question is to follow your heart and your excitement. They will tell you what is next in line for you.

A simple rule of thumb is to go opposite of the masses. Every negative outcome you see, every negative action or word, use them as points of contrast and as triggers to create mentally the experience that you would like in your life. Simultaneously, bless the ill-fated with the same positive outcomes that you have created for yourself. This is the highest of gifts to the world and to yourself.

Corrections In Thinking Yield Corrections In Experience

Minor adjustments in course can equal large changes in trajectory. This is true in aviation and it is true in life. The pilot is constantly making adjustments to his flight pattern as he works to approach his destination. The plane's progress is not a straight line. Even the most minor of degree shift in direction can yield a difference of hundreds of miles from the designated ending point. This seems to be the current course of the human race.

The challenge is not outer experience. This has been established already. The challenge is that the current of thought has fallen deeper into the realm of the lower vibration for so long that few are able to see the availability of other choices. When damned, ill experiences begin to appear to be the norm, greater possibility becomes lost until that one who is willing to be the light, ventures to prove and show that there is more available. Once realized, you recognize that the damned norm is far from the truth, that energy and vibration equal experience, and the choice of energy, the choice of vibration belong to the individual wielder.

The corrections in thought that yield the corrections in experience are chronicled and outlined and passionately delivered. You can be this person. You can be that light. You must merely engage the ideas and processes that are being presented. Whether you believe in them wholeheartedly or not, if you believe in possibility, you will see results first in yourself and second in your experience.

An animal without a master roams the wasteland. Its attention is drawn from one place to the next, based on its drive to secure resources to cover its basic need for survival. The beast will attack, it will cower, it will run, but its position is always based on right now. Its position is always based in surviving the present moment.

The present moment, is a power place of clarity and focus, but it is not a position based on survival. This is the animalistic record of behavior. From the human standpoint, the present moment should be a constant recipient of the wielder's highest thinking. The mind was

34

not designed to wander. It was not designed to be a wild beast leaping from one moment to the next, one experience to the next without any guidance or higher purpose. The mind is meant to be a piercing tool of focus and clarity, a laser like instrument of creation and manifestation. Its ability to summon habits, display discipline, and influence the collective around it warrants incredible acknowledgment and attention.

Corrections on the mental plane are the correction of experience. Your expectation, your perception, each weigh in on your view of life and what and how manifestation appears in front of you.

Corrections on the mental plane create a new aura every time you adjust yourself to the beauty and wonder of the highest experiences you desire. They exist. They are being experienced now. You have just as much right to them as anyone in your history.

Make the necessary corrections inwardly, and the corrections of the outer physical world will take care of themselves.

Truth Is A Facet Of Your Soul, Not A Collective Idea

If the individual human being was meant to be solely a product of the collective thought that surrounds him or her, then there would be no need for this conversation, but since this is not the case, this conversation is absolutely paramount.

Your soul is constantly working to deliver its guidance and suggestion to you. It is constantly attempting to make suggestions to you based on your purpose, based on your truth.

Truth is not a multifaceted thing with a head and tail that if crossed condemns you to a life of inconvenience and suffering. Truth is your calling. It is your unique path and the knowledge available to you as you play to stay in alignment with that path. The signs, they are for you. The detours, they are for you. The people that you meet, they are for you, and their messages, their guidance can only be interpreted by you in the way that is necessary for your personal, individual growth and expansion.

Truth is not a singularity. It is subjective to the individual. It is obvious in your culture. In one culture, importance is given to an idea or a way of doing things, and in another culture it has no meaning at all. Even closer to home, ten, twenty, one hundred years ago ideas or behaviors were unacceptable, and now they are accepted. Yesterday's truth is not today's truth, and change is constantly molding and making, bringing new light to the considerations of the masses. Truth is a highly individualistic function.

So, what is your truth? How important is it to uncover the truth that awaits you? How important is it to awaken the values and the desires that are uniquely yours? Accepting that you have a truth and that it is the most important thing to the fulfillment of your soul's purpose is the first recognition and the awakening of power. You have magic at your disposal. You have a path that beckons your arrival. You have magnificent discoveries about yourself that await you, but it all hinges on your recognizing, accepting, and engaging your truth.

36

Optimally, your life would run simply and clearly without complication, but that is not the case. There are distractions and opportunities that jar your focus if you allow them to do so. There are comfortable paths or choices of inaction that allow you, for a moment, to divert the tug and pull of your soul's calling, but the nudge never fully subsides. It grows, it pressures, it begs for life until life awakens and allows it, or death smothers it. You are its caretaker, whether you want to be or not.

Reflection Is The Basis Of Your Life Experience

In conclusion, it is critical to discuss and demonstrate the fundamental nature of your experience. In dramatic fashion, we could highlight all major points in your life, and take a toll of your inner feelings and makeup during that time to see if the occurrence was something you were truly searching for, or if it was something that you abhorred and were damned if you would participate. We are sure that if you were completely clear and honest that it would not be a shock to find out that the outcome you experienced was already envisioned in your mind and body, either specifically or something akin to its vibration.

So, without further ado, let us conclude that the crux of all humanity, the reality that makes all habitual patterns unnatural, is that your life experiences are a reflection of you. If you start here, drop everything else you have read, and strive to remember your thoughts, your streaming mind activity, and your emotional patterns, you will quickly come to the conclusion that you are the creator.

It also begs a mention that on the physical plane, your creations are somewhat bound by the limits of time and space. Thus come into play the concepts of focus and concentration. However, in the inner energy realms, the moment you think a thought, imagine a new idea, concept, or experience, it is created. It exists, but it is also up to you to continue to feed that idea and allow it to grow until it becomes manifest in the physical realm.

The speed by which manifestation appears is directly related to the amount or lack of mental blockage that you carry. Those things that you do not feel or believe are difficult to accomplish or acquire manifest quickly and easily. Those things that you believe mentally will be difficult to manifest, there is something you must do first, or that someone or something has influence over your outcome, will be difficult for you to manifest. You will not allow it onto the physical plane until the barriers you believe to be in place are moved or have been cleared.

In truth, there are no barriers to your creations, your manifestations, except for those you believe in your heart to be there.

Understanding that your life is a reflection of you is the key concept to start with. Your experiences in relationships with your partner or spouse, with your children, with your parents, and at work, are all a reflection of either the pain or joy that exists inside of you. Chronic sickness and dis-ease within your body are a reflection of the confusion and dis-ease that exist within you mentally. It is also a result of your participation in the low vibrating energies of the realm. Your inability to manifest wealth and abundance in your life is a direct reflection of your self-worth and self-confidence.

Each area of your life is a reflection of your inner makeup. The state of the human race is a direct reflection of the inner makeup of the mass mind. However, because of the strength of vibration, the few who choose to participate in the higher energy vibrations provide counter to the low energy participants of the world, and by adding to the ranks through model and example, the tide can be turned and the field of high vibration can once again cover your world.

On the personal level, which is where it always comes back to, your life is a reflection of you, and it does not take much effort or much time to realize the immense power you wield and the effect and influence you can have on those who pass through your experience.

We honor your having completed this work. We honor your being here, at this place. We honor your arriving at this turning point in your life with a choice to embrace a new position, a new outlook on life, or to discard it. Those who love you and strive to protect you, watch on with reverence and awe. For whatever you choose, the bell will toll, and the call of your soul will eventually bring you back to this place. We care, and we are watching.

With Love Eternal.

Thank You!!

A Few Things You Would Know If You Were God

In Spirit I Thrive, In Mind I Fall. It Is My Job, To Unify Them All.

I now realize that for two decades I have been striving to release the true, authentic me that had been covered by fear-based ideas and perceptions. (Get Past Yourself)

I am realizing that the life I once lived, and the life story that is being lived around me by family and friends is not a chosen life, but one that has been passed along. With elements of fear at its base, loss, pain, failure, and the embarrassment of mistake once defined me, now they propel me. (The Other Side Of Fear)

Now I strive to allow the true, authentic, Source inspired me to breathe through at every moment. This grants me the knowing that my desires are pure and in line with the path that is specifically for me. (Allowing Me)

A Few Things You Would Know If You Were God

I did not need a teacher, a preacher, or a guru. All I needed was some Guidance and some Direction. (My Only Need)

Benny

The Rest Of The Series

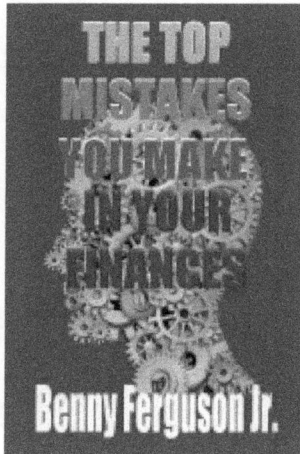

Connecting With Benny:

Facebook: www.facebook.com/bennyrfergusonjr

Youtube: www.youtube.com/BennyFergusonJr/videos

Twitter: www.twitter.com/BennyRFergusonJ

Contacting Benny:

Initial contacts to Benny for discussions, interviews, one – on - one or group coaching, speaking or training may be made through telephone or email.

Phone: 336-546-7142

Email: BennyFerguson@TheFergusonCompany.com